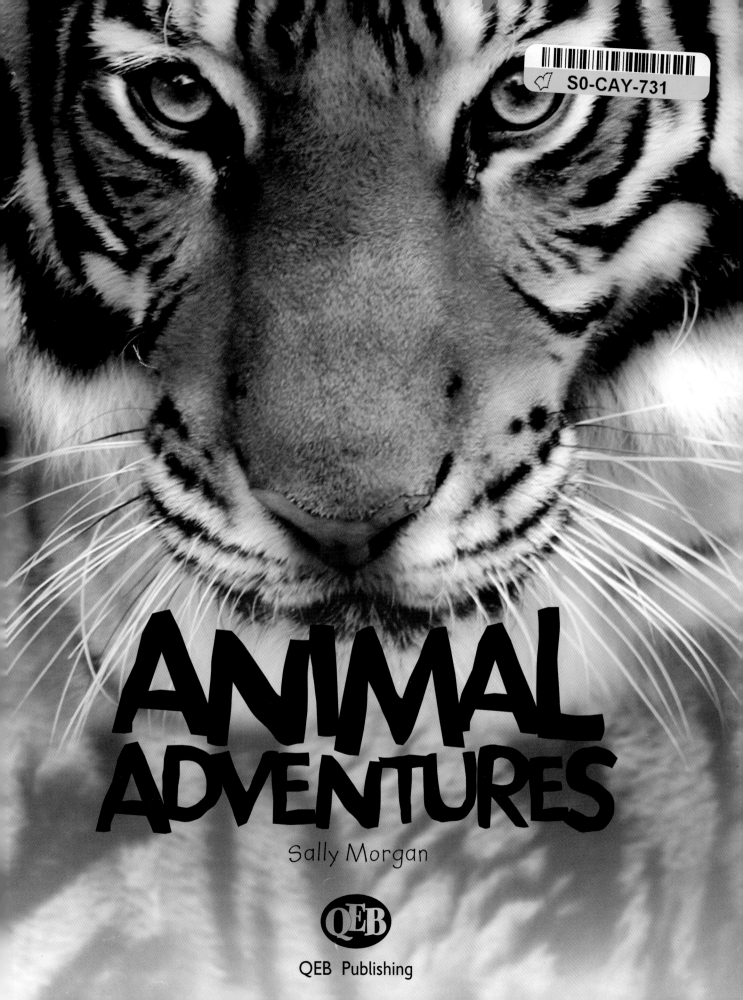

S0-CAY-731

ANIMAL ADVENTURES

Sally Morgan

QEB

QEB Publishing

Copyright © QEB Publishing 2009

Published in the United States by
QEB Publishing, Inc.
3 Wrigley, Suite A
Irvine, CA 92618

www.qed-publishing.co.uk

All rights reserved. No part of this publication may be reproduced, stored in a retrieval system, or transmitted in any form or by any means, electronic, mechanical, photocopying, recording or otherwise, without the prior permission of the publisher, nor be otherwise circulated in any form of binding or cover other than that in which it is published and without a similar condition being imposed on the subsequent purchaser.

Library of Congress Cataloging-in-Publication Data is available from the Library of Congress

Author Sally Morgan
Design and editorial by East River Partnership

ISBN: 978 1 59566 891 2

Printed in China

10 9 8 7 6 5 4 3 2 1

Picture Credits
Key: t = top, b = bottom, l = left, r = right,
c = center, FC = front cover

Ardea 97 Brian Bevan, 99b Steve Hopkin;
Corbis 5r Tom Brakefield, 14 Renee Lynn, 18–19 Jeffrey L. Rotman, 27 Raymond Gehman, 30 Paul A. Souders, 31 zefa, 31 Keren Su, 33 Bryn Colton, 34 Renee Lynn, 38t D Robert & L Franz, 45 Jim Zuckerman, 51t Tim Davis, 56 Bettmann, 58 Joe MacDonald, 60 Klaus Nigge/Foto Natura, 64 Linda Richardson, 65 Kennan Ward, 66–67, 66b Joe McDonald, 68 Tony Hamblin, 69b, 69t Anthony Bannister, 71 George McCarthy, 72 Jonathan Blair, 73 Martin Harvey/Gallo Images, 75t Jonathan Blair, 79t Michael and Patricia Fogden, 83t Jean Hall: Cordaiy Photo Library Ltd, 100–101 Ralph A Clevenger;**Ecoscene** 16–17 Philip Colla, 17 Kelvin Aitken, 23 Gerard Lacz, 28b Michael Gore, 38 Paul Souders, 42 Neeraj Mishra, 52b John Farmar,

78–79 Papilio/Robert Pickett, 78b Papilio/Paul Franklin, 81 Papilio/Robert Picket, 82–83 Papilio/Robert Picket, 83b Papilio/Robert Picket, 4 Philip Colla, 86 Chinch Gryniewicz, 88t V&W Brandon Cole, 89 Philip Colla, 90 Mike Buxton, 91 Robert Pickett, 92 Robert Pickett, 93b Robin Williams, 93t Robert Pickett, 95b Fritz Polking, 98 Robert Pickett, 101t Ken Wilson, 103b Ken Wilson, 103cl, 103br N A Callow, 111 Chinch Gryniewicz, 111t Robin Williams; **FLPA** 5 Hugo Willcox/Foto Natura, 19t Gerard Lacz, 46 Yva Momatiuk & John Eastcott/Minden Pictures, 54–55 Winifried Wisniewski, 57 Derek Middleton, 59 Winifried Wisniewski/Foto Natura, 61b Michio Hoshino/Minden Pictures, 63 Chris Newbert/Minden Pictures, 74–75 Eric Woods, 76–77 Yva Momatiuk/John Eastcott/Minden Pictures, 76t Fritz Polking, 96 Silvestris Fotoservice, 99t Robert Cattlin; **Getty Images** 8–9 Art Wolfe, 10 Ken Lucas, 11 Gallo Images/Heinrich van den burg, 14–15 Tim Davis, 24–25 Taxi, 26 Kathy Bushue, 28–29 David E Myers, 35 Jonathan and Angela, 37 Renee Lynn, 40 Jack Hollingsworth, 41 Daryl Balfour, 43 Johan Elzenga, 48 Johnny Johnson, 49b Art Wolfe, 49t David Hosking, 50–51 Wolfgang Kaehler, 52t David Tippling, 53 Kevin Schafer, 70 Cousteau Society, 85 Jeff Rotman, 87 Jeff Rotman, 88b Jeff Hunter, 110 Kevin Schafer, 112–113 Al Satterwhite, 19b Tony Bennett; **NHPA** 32 Martin Harvey, 44 Kevin Schafer, 62–63 Bill Love; **Photolibrary** 16 Gerard Soury, 22 Pacific Stock/James Watt, 37–37 Renee Lynn, 104–105 Oxford Scientific; **Photoshot/NHPA** 6–7, 16–17 Stephen Dalton, 107t George Bernard; **Shutterstock** 2–3 Styve Reineck background, 4–5 Grigory Kubatyan, 20–21, 80 Graham@theGraphicZone, 102 Marek Lambert, 105t D Morley Read, 105b Arteki, 106 Pixelman; **Still Pictures** 11, 15 Kevin Schafer, N Grainer 33, 55t Ed Reschke,
57 Hans Pfetschinger, 94 J. Venot,
95t Ed Reschke.

Words in **bold** are explained in the Glossary on page 114.

Contents

Bats 4

Apes 8

Whales, dolphins, and porpoises 16

Bears 26

Big cats 30

Elephants 40

Giraffes 44

Penguins 48

Birds of prey 54

Turtles 62

Snakes 66

Alligators and crocodiles 70

Amphibians 78

Sharks 84

Butterflies 90

Bees and wasps 96

Ants 102

Spiders 108

Glossary 114

Index 118

Bats

Bats are **mammals**. These are animals that have hair and give birth to live young. Bats are small creatures that rest and sleep during the day and come out at night to feed. Most bats have furry bodies and a pair of leathery wings with which they can fly silently through the air.

Trees and caves

Bats hang upside-down from trees and the walls of caves rather than coming to rest on the ground.

Bats prefer to roost in caves that are neither too hot nor too cold.

Bat fact!

One of the largest bats is the Bismarck flying fox, which has a wingspan as wide as an adult human is tall.

Roosts

When bats are not flying, they are roosting. A bat's roost is a dry place where it is safe from **predators**. Bat roosts can be found in roof spaces, under bridges, in dark caves, in the branches and hollows of trees, and even under fallen logs.

Bats, along with insects and birds, are the only animals that can fly.

Bat colonies

Most bats live and roost together in a group called a **colony**. As many as 200,000 fruit bats may roost in one tree, while millions of bats can roost in the same cave.

Feeding and hunting

Bats have to eat a lot of food every day. If a bat goes without food for just two days, it may die. Smaller bats feed on **insects**, frogs, mice, and even other bats. Larger fruit bats eat plant food, such as **nectar**, fruits, and bark.

Using sound to "see"

Flying at night, bats make high-pitched sounds that humans cannot hear. These sounds bounce off objects and create echoes. The bat hears these echoes and makes a picture in its brain of where the object is and how big it is. This is called **echolocation**. Bats use it to find their way around and when hunting for food.

Bats can safely fly around obstacles in complete darkness using echolocation.

Feeding on fish

The fish-eating bat flies low over ponds and rivers to feed on fish that are swimming close to the surface of the water. Once it finds a fish, the bat flies lower still so that its hooked claws drag in the water. It then grabs the fish with its claws and bites it through the head.

The greater bulldog bat flies close to the surface of the water in its search for fish.

Bat fact!

The pipistrelle bat may eat as many as 3,000 midges during a feeding session. A colony of these bats eats millions of insects each summer.

Apes

Orangutans and gorillas are apes, which is a type of **primate**. Primates are a group of mammals including lemurs, monkeys, chimpanzees, and humans. They have large brains, good eyesight, and are **adapted** to be able to climb trees. Primates are mammals.

A gorilla is a very strong and powerful animal.

Big bodies

Gorillas are the world's largest primates. They have very long arms, and a bulky body with a broad chest. The males are twice as big as the females. Older males have white hairs on their backs and are called **silverbacks**. Orangutans are intelligent animals that live in **rain forests**. They move around the rainforest by climbing along branches.

Gorilla fact!

The name gorilla means "hairy person" and was first used by an explorer from North Africa 2,500 years ago.

The large body of the orangutan is covered in long, orange-red hair.

Beginning life

Gorilla babies are born at any time of the year. A female gorilla is **pregnant** for 8.5 months. Newborn babies have gray-pink skin and a thin covering of hair. The mother feeds her baby on milk for three years.

The female gorilla feeds her baby with milk that is rich in protein and fat.

Orangutan

A female orangutan is ready to have a baby when she is about ten years old. Newborn babies weigh about 2 pounds (1 kilogram) —that's the same as a bag of sugar.

Carried around

A female orangutan carries her baby everywhere for the first year of its life. At about two months, the baby starts to crawl and can walk at nine months old. The mother continues to carry her youngster on longer journeys until it is four years old.

This baby clings to its mother's fur as she climbs a tree.

Orangutan fact!

A female orangutan has a baby every seven to eight years. She only has two or three babies in her lifetime.

Living together

Living in a group

Gorillas live in family groups of between three and 30 animals. A typical gorilla family consists of one adult male (the silverback), three or four adult females, and five or six youngsters. The most important individual is the silverback, who is head of the group.

Gorilla fact!

When an adult male takes over a family group, he may kill some of the baby gorillas that belonged to the previous silverback.

The ages of family members can range from newborns to more than 30 years old.

Living alone

Orangutans live alone in the rain forest. The only time they live with other orangutans is when they are growing up, when a young female returns to visit her mother, or when a male visits a female to **mate** with her. This is different from other primates, such as chimpanzees and gorillas, who live together in groups.

Orangutans spend most of their lives alone in the trees.

Moving around

Orangutans move slowly from tree to tree, using their very long arms. The length of each arm is about the same as the height of a five-year-old child. The hands and feet of orangutans are hook-shaped to make it easier to grab branches.

Knuckle-walking

Gorillas usually walk on all fours, using both their arms and legs. They put their weight on the knuckles of their fist, not on their palms. This is known as knuckle-walking.

Young orangutans can swing from branch to branch and travel quickly through the forest.

Gorilla fact!

A male gorilla is about 7 inches (15 centimeters) shorter than an average human but its arms are one foot (30 centimeters) longer.

Gorillas can knuckle-walk because they have long arms that reach to the ground.

Whales, dolphins, and porpoises

Marine mammals

Whales, dolphins, and porpoises are mammals. This means that the females give birth to live young and feed them milk. Unlike most other mammals, whales, dolphins, and porpoises do not have body hair. Their skin is sleek, smooth, and rubbery. They belong to a group of mammals called **cetaceans**.

Dolphins and porpoises live in groups called **pods**, which can be very large.

Even large dolphins like to leap out of the water when they swim close to the surface.

Dolphin fact!

Dolphins range in size. The bottlenose dolphin is about 12 feet long (3 meters). Hector's dolphin is 4 feet long (1 meter).

Breathing

Dolphins and porpoises have a fish-like body and flippers, but they do not have **gills** like fish. Instead, they have a pair of lungs, so, unlike fish, they have to come to the surface of the water to breathe.

Largest whale

The largest animal in the world is the blue whale. The blue whale is just one of many types of whales that swim in the world's oceans.

Whales have flippers, a long body, and no back limbs.

Giving birth

A female dolphin is pregnant for one year. She gives birth to one **calf**, which is born tail first. Soon after the birth, she pushes her calf to the water's surface so that it can take its first breath. As dolphins and whales breathe through a **blowhole** on the top of their head, the newborn calf has to learn when to open and close its blowhole to avoid breathing in water!

A newborn bottlenose dolphin calf weighs about 15 to 20 pounds (7 to 9 kilograms) and is up to 3 feet (1 meter) long.

Dolphin fact!

The Indus River dolphin sometimes carries its young on its back, above the surface of the water.

First month

Female whales may be pregnant for between nine and 17 months, depending on the species. Many female whales swim to a special place where they give birth to a single calf.

The calf stays close
to its mother's side

First month

The whale calf feeds on its mother's milk, which helps the calf to grow quickly. During the first month, the calf stays close to its mother's side. Her movements in the water help to pull the calf gently along.

Feeding

Dolphins, porpoises, and toothed whales are **carnivores**, or meat eaters. They mainly eat fish, such as anchovies, mackerel, herring, and cod, as well as squid.

Swallowed whole

Dolphins and porpoises have small, sharp teeth. As they cannot chew, dolphins and porpoises swallow small fish whole. If a fish is too large to swallow whole, dolphins will rip it up and swallow it in chunks. Toothed whales hunt mainly for fish and squid. Their teeth are small and pointed—ideal for gripping slippery **prey**.

This group of humpback whales has found a **shoal** of fish and is busy feeding.

Hunting together

Orcas are dolphins and they hunt together in a pack. They prey on fish and seals, and sometimes the calves of other whales. Orcas gather off the coast of Argentina from October to April to feed off seal pups.

Filter feeding

Baleen whales eat plankton, **krill**, and small fish. Hundreds of plates hang from the whale's upper jaw. The whale swallows water and forces it through the plates, trapping food contained in the water.

Dolphins trap small fish between their teeth and then swallow them whole.

Dolphin fact!

A bottlenose dolphin eats 44 pounds (20 kilograms) of fish a day—the weight of 12 chickens.

Living in pods

Most pods contain about ten dolphins or porpoises, although the biggest pods can have many thousands of animals in them. A typical pod is made up of mothers and their calves together with a few bulls.

Hunting together

When hunting, a pod communicates by whistling. Sometimes, pods join together to form large hunting herds. If a mother joins a hunting group, her calves are often looked after by other females in the pod.

This pod of spinner dolphins is made up males, females, and calves.

Young orcas, or killer whales, are very playful. They jump out of the water and twist in mid-air.

Migration

Many whales make long journeys each year. They spend part of the year eating in cold water and then swim to warmer waters where the female whales give birth to their calves. This annual trip is called **migration**.

Why do they migrate?

Whales swim to warmer waters because their cold-water feeding areas freeze over, and they prefer to give birth in warm water. Calves do not have a thick layer of **blubber** like adults, so they could not survive in cold water.

Whale fact!

Gray whales migrate the furthest—as much as 12,700 miles (20,400 kilometers) each year, from the Arctic to Mexico and back again.

Senses

Whales, dolphins, and porpoises use their senses to find their way around and catch their prey. They cannot smell, but their hearing is incredibly sensitive. They do not have ears like humans, instead there are two tiny openings on the side of their head, which lead to ears inside their **skull**.

The tiny eyes of this blue whale are behind its mouth. Whales are used to living in murky water, where they can see objects only up to about 3 feet (one meter) away.

Echolocation

Dolphins, whales, and porpoises can "see" in water using sound. This is called echolocation and is similar to **sonar** used by submarines. They produce lots of whistles and clicks, which bounce off objects and return as an echo. By listening to the echoes, they can figure out the shape and position of objects, including prey.

Communication

Whales communicate in many ways. They make sounds such as whistles, trills, moans, and squeals. These sounds travel great distances through the water. **Breaching** and lobtailing (slapping their tails on the surface) are other ways whales communicate.

Whale fact!

Submarines find their way around the oceans using a form of echolocation, called sonar.

Bears

Bears are mammals. They have large feet called paws, with long, sharp claws. Bears are covered with fur. This helps them to stay warm, even when the temperature around them is very cold.

Cubs

A female bear is pregnant for eight months. A newborn cub is small, about the size of a guinea pig. Cubs are born blind and without fur. They **suckle** their mother's milk for six months before they start to eat solid food.

A female bear gives birth to a **litter** of one to three cubs.

Dens

Bears that live in cold climates spend the winter in a **den**. Their cubs are born in the den in the middle of winter. In spring, the bear leads her cubs outside for the first time. Black and brown bears in colder parts of the world spend the winter in a deep sleep, called **hibernation**. Polar bears do not hibernate. They are active all year round.

A female American black bear and her cub have crawled under a large log to hibernate.

Bear fact!

It is not unusual for a bear to lose one-third of its body weight while it is hibernating.

Hunters

Polar bears and brown bears are predators. They have sharp teeth and long claws to grip their prey. The polar bear is a carnivore and hunts for its prey.

Charging and waiting

Sometimes the polar bear will charge toward its prey. At other times, it sits beside a hole in the ice, waiting for a seal to come up to breathe. When the seal comes up, the bear bites it and drags it onto the ice.

A seal provides enough food to feed
a polar bear for about eight days.

Fishing for food

Brown bears feed on a variety of food, such as fish, insects, and berries. They are called **omnivores**. In the fall, they fish in rivers. The bears wade into the water and catch salmon as they swim past. The young cubs practice by standing in shallow water, trying to catch the salmon.

Brown bears grip the slippery salmon in their claws or teeth.

Bear fact!

A brown bear can eat up to 35 pounds (16 kilograms) of food each day.

Big cats

Lions, tigers, and cheetahs are all mammals called big cats. Big cats are carnivores—they eat meat—and are skilful hunters.

Lions

A male lion has a thick mane around his head. A female lion is called a lioness, and her young are called cubs. Lions live in families called prides.

Male lions are about 10 feet (3 meters) long. A lioness is slightly smaller.

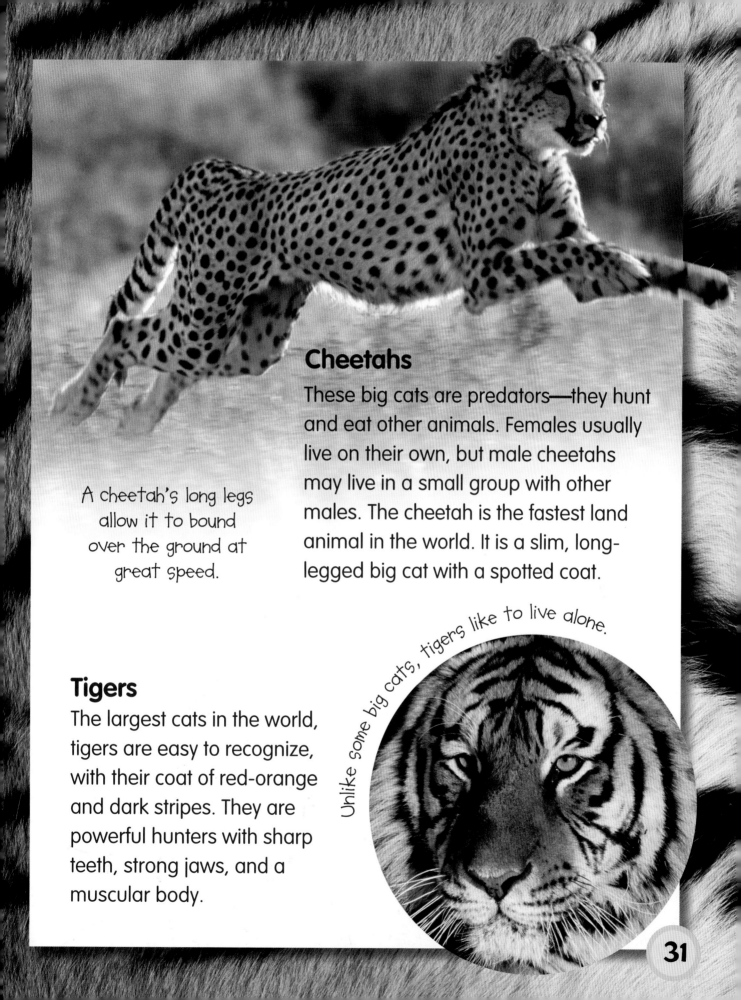

Cheetahs

These big cats are predators—they hunt and eat other animals. Females usually live on their own, but male cheetahs may live in a small group with other males. The cheetah is the fastest land animal in the world. It is a slim, long-legged big cat with a spotted coat.

A cheetah's long legs allow it to bound over the ground at great speed.

Tigers

The largest cats in the world, tigers are easy to recognize, with their coat of red-orange and dark stripes. They are powerful hunters with sharp teeth, strong jaws, and a muscular body.

Unlike some big cats, tigers like to live alone.

Beginning life

Lions, tigers, and cheetahs are pregnant for three to four months. There are normally two or three cubs in a litter and the mother feeds the cubs with her milk for the first six months. Newborn big cat cubs are about the size of a house cat. They are born helpless and they cannot walk. They only open their eyes after about ten days.

These cubs are suckling milk from their mother.

Often, one of the tiger cubs dies shortly after birth. This is usually the smallest cub, called the runt.

Living in a pride

Lions live in groups called prides. A typical pride is made up of between four and 12 lionesses, their cubs, and up to six adult males. The lionesses are all related, but none of them are related to the pride's adult males.

This lioness is carrying her cub to a safe place.

When the cubs have eaten, the mother licks them clean.

Growing up

Playing helps cubs to learn hunting and fighting skills. When they are about one year old, the mothers allow cubs to follow them on a hunt. At first the youngsters only watch, but they quickly learn how to chase and catch their own prey.

Growing and learning

By the time they are a year old, the male cubs are much larger than the females. As they get older, the cubs become braver and may spend a whole day alone. By the time they are two years old, the cubs can live on their own.

Play-fighting is important as it helps young cubs learn to hunt.

Cheetah fact!

Only about one cheetah cub in every ten survives to three months. Some are killed by lions and hyenas, others die from disease and lack of food.

A lioness takes young cubs to feed after a hunt.

Learning to survive

The mother leaves her cubs when they are 14 to 18 months old. The female cubs stay in roughly the same area, but the males move far away to find a new **territory**.

Movement

Although an adult cheetah can reach a top speed of about 60 miles an hour (100 kilometers an hour) when it needs to, it usually runs at a slower 35 miles an hour (55 kilometers an hour) when chasing after its prey.

Built for speed

The cheetah's slim body, long legs, and bendy back are built for speed. It can take long strides and move across the ground quickly. Large lungs allow the cheetah to breathe plenty of air, and a long tail provides balance when changing direction.

Charge!

Lions can charge at speeds of 30 miles an hour (50 kilometers an hour) for a short distance. They can also leap 30 feet (9 meters)—almost as long as a bus. A lioness can run faster than a male lion.

Jumping and swimming

All cats walk on their toes. Tigers can move extremely fast over short distances, but they can't keep this speed up for very long. Tigers are also powerful swimmers. In South East Asia, tigers spend a lot of their time in rivers or swamps, hunting fish and turtles.

The back legs of the tiger are longer than its front legs. This means they can jump large distances.

These cheetahs are seen at full stretch as they lift all four legs off the ground while running fast.

Lion fact!

Lions have five toes on their front paws and four toes on their back paws.

Predators

Big cats are carnivores, or meat eaters, and are strong enough to kill prey that is as large as they are. Their claws are long, strong, and curved, and hook into a victim's flesh.

An adult tiger has 30 teeth.

Closer and closer

A cheetah hunts by stalking its prey, sometimes for many hours at a time. It creeps closer and closer until it is ready to attack. The cheetah's spotted coat helps it to move in long grass without being seen.

This cheetah family is bringing down a Thomson's gazelle.

Hunting together

When lionesses work together, they can kill large prey, such as zebras. A large animal can feed a pride for several days. At the start of a hunt, the lionesses spread out. Some walk toward the prey, forcing it near the other lionesses that are hidden in the grass. These lionesses ambush the prey when it is close enough.

Lionesses creep up slowly on their prey. They are very patient and may stalk prey for hours.

Lion fact!

A lion's tongue is like sandpaper. It is used to scrape bits of meat off bones.

Hunting at night

Tigers hunt alone and at night, preying on large, hoofed mammals, such as deer and pigs. When a tiger finds prey, it eats until it is full, and then covers the remains with leaves and soil. It returns when it is hungry to feed some more. A tiger needs to kill once a week, but a female tiger with cubs has to find food every five or six days.

Elephants

The elephant has a huge, gray body, strong legs, and a long **trunk**. It also has large, flapping ears. Most elephants have tusks, too. These are extra-long teeth, which continue to grow through the elephant's life. The male elephant is called a bull and the female is called a **cow**.

Elephant fact!

The elephant is the largest living land animal.

A fully grown female elephant uses her trunk to feed on grass.

Trunks

An elephant uses its trunk to smell. The trunk is formed from the elephant's nose and upper lip. There are two nostrils that run down the whole trunk. Smell helps to keep the herd together. It allows elephants to detect predators, such as lions or tigers. At the first hint of danger, an elephant raises its trunk to smell the air.

Elephants can pick up very small objects with the end of their trunks, in the same way that we use our fingertips.

Growing up

A female elephant is pregnant for 22 months. She gives birth to only one baby, called a calf. A newborn calf has reddish hair over its head and back. It gradually loses this hair as it gets older. The calf feeds on its mother's milk for the first three years of its life. Then it starts to eat grass and other plants.

Elephant fact!

A newborn elephant calf weighs between 170–250 pounds (77–115 kilos). It stands about 1 yard (0.9 meters) high from the ground to its shoulder.

An Asian elephant calf with its mother.

Herds

Female elephants live in family groups called herds. A typical herd is made up of three or four adult females and their calves. All the adult females are related. The herd is led by the oldest female. She is called the matriarch. The herd gets larger as more calves are born, so some of the females may leave and form their own herd.

Young elephants learn by watching their mothers and the other members of the herd.

Giraffes

Giraffes are mammals. They are the tallest animal in the world. They could look into a second-floor window without even having to stand on tiptoe! They have incredibly long necks and four long legs. Their coats have a pattern of brown patches on a lighter yellowish background.

Each giraffe has its own unique pattern of markings.

Giraffe fact!

The tongue of the giraffe is very long. It is about 18 inches (46 centimeters)— that's as long as a child's arm!

Feeding

Giraffes are plant eaters, or **herbivores**. They are browsing animals that feed on the leaves of trees. Often, trees have long thorns to stop browsing animals from eating their leaves. However, the giraffes pull the leaves and thorns into their mouths. Then they produce lots of saliva to help chew and swallow the thorny mixture.

You can tell a bull from a cow by the way it eats. Cows tend to bend their necks, while bulls eat at full stretch.

45

Beginning life

A female giraffe is ready to have her first calf when she is about five years old. After mating, she is pregnant for about 15 months. Giraffes give birth to one calf at a time. Twin calves are very rare.

Growing tall

A newborn calf weighs about 220 pounds (100 kilograms) and is just under 6.5 feet (2 meters) tall—that's as tall as an adult man! Calves grow quickly—some double their height in just one year.

A newborn calf can stand up, walk, and run within an hour of birth.

Living in herds

Giraffes live in a group called a herd. The herds are made up of individuals of one sex, for example the cows and their young, or a group of young bulls. There are usually between 12 and 15 animals in a herd.

Giraffe fact!

Giraffes have less sleep than almost any other mammal—between 20 minutes and two hours in every 24 hours.

Living in a herd helps to protect the giraffes against predators.

Penguins

It is easy to recognize a penguin, with its black back and white front. Penguins are plump, with short legs and **webbed** feet.

Birds

Penguins belong to a group of animals called birds. Birds are covered in feathers and they reproduce by laying eggs. The penguin is different from most birds, as it cannot fly. However, it is an excellent swimmer and can even sleep on water!

These King penguins have a black back and a white front.

Living in colonies

Penguins like to be close to other penguins. When they are on land, penguins live together in large groups called colonies. Colonies vary in size and can have 400 or 40,000 penguins in them. There are about 40 different Emperor penguin colonies in the Antarctic.

Penguins return to the same place each year to breed.

A huge colony of King penguins.

penguin fact!

Some of the largest Chinstrap colonies have more than one million penguins in them.

Laying eggs

Penguins come onto land to mate and breed. Most penguins lay their eggs in a simple nest made of feathers, grass, or even a pile of rocks.

Incubating the eggs

Penguins only lay one or two eggs. The eggs are **incubated** by both parents. They take turns looking after the eggs over a period of about two months.

penguin fact!

Of the two eggs laid by penguins, often only one chick **hatches**. Sometimes both hatch but only one survives.

A penguin kindergarten can be very large with many hundreds of chicks tightly packed together.

Growing up

A newly hatched chick nestles under its parent to keep warm. One parent stays with the chick while the other feeds in the sea. Older chicks are left in kindergarten groups while both their parents feed. Leaving the chicks in a group provides more protection from predators and from the cold.

Adult penguins will only recognize and feed their own chicks.

Daily life

Penguins feed mostly on fish, squid, and krill. Each penguin species has a beak designed to catch its prey. King penguins have a long, curved beak, which is ideal for catching large squid. The Humboldt penguin has a short, thick beak for catching small fish, such as sardines and anchovies.

Many penguins feed on krill.

The King penguin has a much longer, thinner beak than other penguins.

Hunting

Most penguins feed during the day. They have two ways of hunting. Sometimes they swim under the ice to find shoals of fish and krill. They also dive deep to catch squid and deep-sea fish.

Walking and swimmimg

The penguin's body is **streamlined**, and is the perfect design for swimming. Penguins use their wings like flippers to swim through the water. Their webbed feet act like paddles when floating on the surface, and as rudders for steering when the penguins are underwater.

Penguins leap into, and out of, the water.

penguin fact!

The Emperor penguin can dive to 1,740 feet (530 meters) to catch fish and squid, staying underwater for 20 minutes at a time.

Birds of prey

Birds of prey are large birds that hunt other animals for food. Eagles, hawks, falcons, owls, and vultures all belong to this group.

Hunting tools

Eagles hunt using their powerful hooked beak, excellent eyesight, and feet that end in curved **talons**. Male and female eagles look similar, although the females are usually larger than the males.

Eagle fact!

The word eagle comes from the **Latin** word "aquila," the name given to the golden eagle by the Romans.

This large Verreaux's eagle has a **wingspan** of more than 6.5 feet (2 meters).

The great horned owl is named after the tufts of feathers on its ears.

In the dark

Many people have heard the sound of an owl hooting at night, but it is unusual to see an owl in the wild. This is because most owls fly at night. Owls perch upright and have a large, round head, a short tail, a hooked beak, and powerful claws called talons. Male and female owls look alike, but females are often larger.

Building a nest

Eagles build huge nests, called **eyries**, in places that are hard to reach, such as on ledges or high in trees. Eagle nests are made from twigs. The inside is lined with soft grass or leaves.

Eagle eggs

The female eagle lays between one and three eggs, and sits on them to keep them warm. The eggs hatch after about 60 days. The egg that was laid first is the first chick to hatch.

Usually the male eagle collects the twigs and the female arranges them in the nest.

Eagle fact!

Up to 90 per cent of all eagle chicks die before they become adults. Some fall to their deaths and others are killed by predators or die from disease.

Owl nests

Male and female owls often stay together for a long time and use the same nest year after year. Some owls' nests have been used for more than 20 years.

Barn owls like to nest on ledges inside large buildings, such as barns.

Owl eggs

Owls breed once a year. A female may lay between two and seven eggs. The mother sits on the eggs for up to five weeks before the chicks are ready to hatch. During this time, she never leaves the nest and is fed by the male owl.

Owl chicks are born with a covering of soft, fluffy feathers.

In the air

Eagles are experts at flying. Their wings are long and wide, which helps them to glide. Many eagles can stay in the air for hours and hardly have to flap their wings at all.

Rising high

Eagles rise high into the sky using **thermals**. These are currents of warm air that rise up from the land. Eagles can fly over long distances using thermals. They are pushed up by one thermal and then slowly glide down to catch the next thermal, which takes them back up again.

The eagle's wing feathers are separated at the tips. This helps air to pass over the wing and makes the eagle's flight smoother.

Silent flying

Most birds make a flapping noise when they fly, caused by the air rushing over the surface of their wings. Owls' wings are different. The soft feathers at the front edge muffle the sound and allow the owls to swoop silently on their prey.

The snowy owl flies in daylight, making short trips from perch to perch.

Owl fact!

Some owls that hunt at night use **camouflage** to blend in with their surroundings while they rest during the day.

Hunting

Eagles hunt during the day using their excellent sight. Some eagles sit at the top of a tree or on a cliff ledge, watching for prey. They stay perfectly still so that their prey does not notice them. When it spots something, the eagle dives down and grabs it.

Eagle fact!

The bateleur eagle spends most of the day in the air. It takes off in the morning and flies until the cooler hours of the evening.

This Steller's sea-eagle has spotted a fish in the water and is about to take off from its perch.

Searching for prey

Owls that live in open habitats, such as grassland or desert, fly slowly, looking for small animals. Sometimes they will crisscross the same piece of land over and over again to make sure they do not miss their prey.

Watching and waiting

Woodland owls sit still in the treetops, watching and listening for small animals moving on the ground below. As soon as they spot their prey, they swoop down to snatch their victim.

This snowy owl has carried its prey back to the nest to feed its young.

Turtles

Turtles are **ancient** animals that first appeared on Earth more than 200 million years ago, when the dinosaurs were alive. They are **reptiles**. Reptiles are animals that have scaly skin. Turtles are easy to recognize because they have a heavy shell covering their back.

This Cagle's map turtle has a flatter shell than a tortoise.

Turtle fact!

The largest turtle is the giant leatherback. Its shell can be up to 8 feet (2.4 meters) long and it can weigh up to 1,900 pounds (867 kilograms).

Adult green turtles are unusual as they feed only on plants such as algae and sea grass.

Feeding

Turtles do not have any teeth. Instead, they have a beaklike structure around their strong jaws. Turtles eat mostly leaves, fruit, and slow-moving animals, such as snails and worms. Sea turtles eat a variety of animal foods including jellyfish, coral, sea urchins, crabs, and fish.

Beginning life

Turtles lay leathery eggs. The female turtle lays between one and 240 eggs at a time, depending on her species. The time taken for the eggs to hatch also varies, from two months to more than a year.

Nesting on beaches

Female sea turtles return to the beach on which they were born to lay their eggs in a hole in the sand. The eggs hatch a few months later, and the **hatchlings** dig their way to the surface. Most hatchlings come out at night and dash to the sea. Some sea turtles lay several **clutches** of eggs each year.

These hatchlings have made it to the safety of the water.

Growing up

Hatchling range in size from just one inch (2.5 centimeters) to about 3 inches (8 centimeters) long. They are on their own from the moment they hatch because their parents do not look after them. Many of the young turtles die during their first few years. A lot are eaten by predators, and others die through a lack of food. Young turtles living in dry habitats may also die during droughts.

Turtle fact!

Many sea turtles die in their first year of life. Only one leatherback turtle in 1,000 survives to adulthood.

It takes these desert tortoises five years to grow to a length of just 3 inches (8 centimeters.)

Snakes

Snakes belong to a group of animals called reptiles. Other reptiles include lizards, crocodiles, and turtles. Most reptiles have four legs and a long tail. But snakes don't have legs—instead they have a very long backbone. This allows them to bend in any direction and even tie themselves into coils and knots.

On land and in water

Most snakes live on land. They burrow into sand and under rocks, and others live in the branches of trees. In some warm parts of the world, snakes swim in water. Snakes, such as the olive sea snake, live out at sea all the time and never see dry land.

Sea snakes have flattened tails that they use as paddles.

snake fact!

The common egg-eater snake swallows bird eggs that are up to four times the size of its head. That's like a person swallowing a car tire.

Live bearers

Some snakes do not lay eggs. Instead, the eggs develop inside the mother's body. The young snakes hatch out from the eggs while they are still inside their mother. The mother then gives birth to them. These snakes are called live bearers.

The female eyelash viper gives birth to live young that are small versions of the adult snakes.

Baby snakes

Newly hatched snakes look like minature versions of the adults. Their parents do not look after them, so the young snakes have to move to a safe place and find food by themselves.

Alligators and crocodiles

This Australian freshwater crocodile has extra-large scales along its back.

Alligators and crocodiles are fierce predators that live near water and are the largest of the world's reptiles. Most reptiles, including alligators and crocodiles, lay eggs that have leathery shells.

Appearance

Alligators and crocodiles look very similar. They both have long bodies and tails, which are covered in thick scales, and legs that stick out to the sides. Most alligators and crocodiles are between 6 and 10 feet (1.8 and 3 meters) in length. The males are much larger than the females.

Crocodile fact!

Crocodiles have an extra reflective layer at the back of their eye so they can see more at night.

Both crocodiles and alligators, such as this American alligator, have a long snout with powerful jaws.

Eggs

Female alligators or crocodiles lay between ten and 50 leathery eggs in a nest. Some species dig out a nest in the ground, but others make a mound by using their feet to gather up dirt. Then they lay their eggs inside the mound. By laying her eggs either in the ground or in a mound of dirt, the female makes sure the eggs stay warm.

This Nile crocodile is laying her eggs in a hole in the ground.

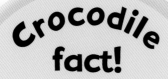

Crocodile fact!

If baby crocodiles are in danger, the mother flips them into her mouth for protection.

Ready to hatch

The eggs remain in the nest for between two and three months. Just before hatching, the young alligators or crocodiles inside the eggs make lots of high-pitched sounds. These sounds tell the mother that they are about to hatch. She digs up the nest to help her hatchlings get to the surface.

Hatchlings break out of their eggs by using a special egg tooth at the end of their jaw.

Hatchlings

Sometimes a hatchling can't break out of its egg. The mother takes the egg gently in her mouth and rolls it backward and forward on her tongue. This opens the shell and allows the hatchling to break free.

Crocodile fact!

Young crocodiles and alligators can climb over obstacles that are several feet high.

Out of every 35 American alligator hatchlings, only six will survive the first year.

Once they have hatched, the mother picks up the hatchlings and carries them to water.

Staying together

The hatchlings stay together after they have hatched. During the day, they spread out to look for food, such as insects and small fish. The hatchlings stay with their mother for several months. Young American alligators stay close to their mother for up to two years. When they leave their mother, the young adults move out into the surrounding area.

Hunting

Alligators and crocodiles feed on a wide range of animals. Most lie in wait for their prey to pass close by. Some alligators and crocodiles float in the water, while others hide in the vegetation that lies at the water's edge.

This Nile crocodile has caught a gazelle.

Powerful jaws

Alligators and crocodiles grab their prey in their jaws and use their jaws to crush the body of the animal that they have caught. Usually the prey is drowned because the alligator or crocodile dives underwater with its catch.

This crocodile leaps out of the water where buffalo are drinking.

Digestion

Alligators and crocodiles swallow their prey whole or break it up into large pieces. They do not have to eat every day because their bodies use up energy slowly. This means they can survive for several months without food, especially in cooler weather, when they are not so active.

Amphibians

Frogs and toads are amphibians. An amphibian is an animal that lives both on land and in water. The word amphibian comes from the Greek words *amphi*, which means "both," and *bios*, which means "life." Newts and salamanders are also amphibians.

Frog or toad?

Most frogs have smooth, moist skin and long back legs, which they use for leaping. Toads, on the other hand, have drier, bumpy skin and shorter back legs, which are better for crawling. Neither frogs nor toads have tails.

The cane toad can grow to be the size of a soccer ball.

Most frogs, such as this tree frog, have a wide mouth and bulging eyes.

Frog and toad food

Frogs and toads are predators. This means that they hunt and eat animals and insects. Their prey includes spiders, earthworms, and even other frogs and toads.

Frog fact!

The goliath frog, at up to 15 inches (38 centimeters) long, is the world's largest frog.

Frogs are found in damp places as they have a moist skin that loses water easily.

Laying eggs

Frogs and toads come together to mate. The female lays her eggs, which are then fertilized by the male.

Frogspawn and long chains

Frog and toad eggs are 2 to 3 millimeters across and contain a tiny embryo surrounded by a coat of protective jelly. Most frogs and toads lay their eggs in clumps or chains. The common frog, for example, lays a large clump of eggs called frogspawn, while the common toad lays its eggs in long chains.

After mating in the spring, the common frog lays its eggs in ponds.

Eggs on leaves

Most frogs and toads lay their eggs in water. Tree frogs, however, lay their eggs on leaves, while other frogs carry their eggs around with them. The male Darwin's frog, for example, keeps eggs in a pouch in its throat. The male midwife toad winds a chain of eggs around its legs and carries them until they hatch.

This glass frog has laid a clump of eggs on a leaf.

Toad fact!

Many toads and frogs return to the pond in which they were born to lay their eggs.

Tadpoles

The eggs of frogs and toads hatch into tiny larvae called tadpoles. These tadpoles have a small, oval body and a long tail.

Gills

When it first hatches, a tadpole uses feathery gills on the outside of its body to breathe underwater. After a while, these gills disappear and the tadpole starts to breathe through new gills inside its body.

Changing body

First, a tadpole's body becomes slimmer. The tail gets shorter until it disappears. Inside, the gills are replaced by lungs that can breathe air. Once this happens, the young frog or toad is ready to crawl onto land.

The back legs of the tadpole of a common frog appear after about eight weeks.

The eggs of the common frog hatch after about 12 days. Eggs from tree frogs hatch after only two days.

This common frog tadpole is about 12 weeks old and now has four legs.

Sharks

Sharks are some of the most amazing creatures in the ocean. Sharks are a type of fish. On the top of their backs, sharks have a large, triangle-shaped fin that sticks up out of the water when they swim near the surface. They have two large **pectoral fins**, one on each side of their body, behind the gill slits.

This blue shark has five gill slits on each side of its head.

Shark teeth

A shark's teeth can be big or small, sharp or blunt, jagged or smooth. The shape of its teeth depends on the type of food it eats. Flat teeth are suitable for crunching snails, crabs, and sea urchins, and jagged teeth are ideal for chewing larger animals.

shark fact!

The great white shark has about 3,000 teeth over its lifetime in its huge mouth.

As sharks get older, their teeth get larger—the oldest sharks have the largest teeth.

Beginning life

A female shark produces only a few large-sized eggs. Most sharks keep their eggs safely inside their body until they are ready to give birth to live young. But some sharks lay their eggs outside their body, and each egg is protected by a tough case.

The dogfish shark's egg attaches itself to rocks or seaweed so that it does not float off into deep water.

Growing up

As soon as shark pups are born, they swim away from their mother. It is important that they leave the parent quickly because some female sharks eat their own pups Sharks grow slowly and may take many years to become a full-sized adult. They then continue to grow throughout their life.

Sharks gradually get larger as they get older.

shark fact!

The spiny shark is thought to live for up to 100 years.

87

Predators

Sharks are predators. This means that they hunt and eat other animals in order to survive. Although sharks eat a variety of foods, their diet is mainly made up of fish and **invertebrates**, such as squid. The larger sharks can catch bigger prey, including turtles, seals, and even dolphins.

A horn shark feeds on a meal of squid eggs on the sea floor.

The large shark is surrounded by smaller fish. Fish are a favourite food of sharks.

Hunting

Sharks hunt in different ways and many attack their prey from below. The hungry shark lurks in the deep water, before it races after its prey at great speed, charging upward out of the darkness of the deep.

shark fact!

Some of the fast sharks can cut through the water at speeds of up to 40 miles (65 kilometers) per hour.

Pack hunting

Although most sharks hunt alone, a few species hunt in packs. Groups of sand tiger sharks, for example, herd shoals of fish into shallow water where they can attack them more easily. Shark pups have to learn to hunt on their own, and many die before they are fully grown.

Some sharks lie in wait for their prey.

Butterflies

Butterflies are insects that can be easily recognized by their large, colorful wings. They can often be seen around flowers.

Butterfly bodies

Butterflies have three body parts—a head, a middle part called a **thorax**, and at the end a part called an **abdomen**. Their eyes and **antennae** are attached to the head. Insects also have three pairs of legs and, usually, two pairs of wings.

A butterfly's wings can be different shapes.

Butterfly food

Adult butterflies do not eat, they only drink. They stay alive by sipping nectar from flowers. Nectar is full of sugar and provides the butterfly with the energy it needs to fly. A butterfly sucks up nectar using a long feeding tube from its mouth called a **proboscis**. Butterflies coil up their proboscis under their head when not feeding.

Butterfly fact!

Some butterflies drink sap that oozes out of the bark of trees.

Butterflies prefer to feed on bright flowers that have wide, flat tops.

Butterfly eggs

After butterflies mate, the female lays her eggs. The eggs have to be laid on a plant that the **caterpillars** can eat. If it is the wrong plant, the caterpillars will starve. Most eggs hatch after about eight days.

From caterpillar to chrysalis

When the caterpillar reaches full size, it stops feeding. It **molts** and begins its **chrysalis** stage. Some caterpillars spin a protective **cocoon** of silk threads around themselves before this stage begins.

Female butterflies, such as this blue morpho, choose the spot to lay their eggs very carefully.

From chrysalis to butterfly

Inside the chrysalis, the caterpillar's body is changing into the shape of an adult butterfly. This is called **metamorphosis** and may take a few days or a couple of months. Soon, the outer skin splits, and an adult butterfly pushes out. Its wings are crumpled up, blood is pumped into them so they expand and dry out. Then the new butterfly is ready to fly away.

The shape of the adult blue morpho butterfly can be seen through the wall of this chrysalis.

Butterfly fact!

Only one in every 100 eggs survives and hatches; the rest are eaten or killed by diseases.

Like all caterpillars, this swallowtail has a body made up of many segments.

Butterfly camouflage

Butterflies have many ways of avoiding being eaten. One way is to blend in with the background so they are difficult to see. This is called camouflage. For example, the comma butterfly has wings with a ragged edge. This shape helps it blend in with spiky plants and undergrowth.

Butterfly fact!

The caterpillars of the orchard swallowtail butterfly are camouflaged to look like bird droppings.

The green coloring of this caterpillar helps it blend in with the colors of the plant stem.

The yellow, orange, and black wings of the monarch butterfly are a warning that it is poisonous.

Poisonous protection

Some butterflies and caterpillars are poisonous and this protects them from predators. They have brightly colored wings to warn hunters that they are not good to eat. The main warning colors used are usually red, yellow, and black.

The wings of this deadleaf butterfly are shaped and colored to look like dead leaves.

95

Bees and wasps

Bees and wasps are brightly colored insects, and most of them sting! Insects are invertebrates, which means they do not have a backbone.

Bee or wasp?

Bees and wasps can be identified by the narrow waist between the thorax and the abdomen, something not found in other insects. It can be difficult to tell a bee from a wasp because they look similar, but bees have a hairy body and legs, while wasps have far fewer hairs.

Bees gather **pollen** and put it into pollen baskets on their legs.

Feeding

Bees visit flowers to collect nectar and pollen. They have a long tongue with a "honey spoon" at the end, which they use to sip up the nectar. Back at the nest, the nectar is passed to other worker bees who store it in cells. The water evaporates from the nectar, leaving a thick, honey syrup.

Wasp fact!

Wasps feed on garden pests such as aphids, whiteflies, and houseflies, which damage plants.

These wasps are feeding on the sugary juices of a plum.

Eggs and larvae

Bees and wasps lay eggs. A bee egg is just 0.05 inches (1.3 millimeters) long, about half the size of a grain of rice. A few days after the egg is laid, a **larva** hatches out. The larva looks like a small, white caterpillar. The larvae eat a lot and grow bigger.

Bee fact!

Honeybees beat their wings more than 230 times per second—this is what creates the buzzing sound of the bee.

The walls of the cells are thin, but can support many times their own weight.

Metamorphosis

When the larva is fully grown, it becomes a **pupa**. During this stage the larva changes into an adult bee or wasp. This change is called metamorphosis. It takes about eight to ten days before the adult insect emerges from the pupa.

These are the pupae of honeybees. Their bodies are changing to become adults.

A queen bee's body is much longer than the bodies of other bees.

Colonies

Social bees and wasps live together in groups called colonies. Each member of the colony has a particular job to do. In a honeybee colony, there are three types of bees—queens, drones, and workers. There is usually one queen. She is the largest bee and lays all the eggs.

Building homes

Honeybees and social wasps are expert home builders. They build complex nests in which they lay their eggs. Honeybees make their home from wax, while wasps chew wood into a pulp which they use to build their nest.

Bees' nests

A bees' nest contains hanging structures called combs, which are made of wax. Each comb is made up of units called cells. The cells contain eggs, larvae, pupae, and stockpiles of pollen and honey. As the nest gets larger, it includes more and more combs.

Bee fact!

Honeybees produce beeswax from the underside of their abdomens.

The walls of the cells are thin but can support many times their own weight.

When a wasp builds its nest, it starts with a stalk hanging from a ceiling or overhead support.

Wasps' nests

A wasps' nest is started by the queen, who lays a few eggs that hatch into worker bees. The workers build the cone-shaped nest and it gradually gets larger, often reaching the size of a soccer ball. The entrance hole is at the bottom.

Ants

Ants are extremely busy insects that live together in groups called colonies. There are more ants in the world than any other type of insect.

Powerful jaws

An ant has a pair of powerful jaws called **mandibles,** and two antennae. An ant uses its antennae for many things, including touching, smelling, and tasting. An ant passes through four stages while developing into an adult. These stages are egg, larva, pupa, and adult.

Ants have a head, a thorax, an abdomen, and six legs.

Ant fact!

Incredibly, the weight of all the ants in the world is equal to the weight of all humans.

Antenna

Head

Thorax

Waist

Leg

Abdomen

Eggs and larvae

At just 0.5 millimeters long, many ant eggs are no bigger than pinheads. The eggs are moist and stick together, which helps worker ants carry them to safety if predators attack the nest. After the eggs are laid by the queen, a larva emerges from each egg. By metamophosis, the larva grows to full size and then changes into a pupa. An adult ant develops inside each pupa.

Eggs

Larva

Pupa

Ant eggs hatch into maggot-like larvae.

Living together

Ants live in colonies of many different sizes. A colony of black ants, for example, contains about 4,000 ants, while a wood ant colony can have 300,000 or more ants. Some of the largest colonies are made up of many millions of ants.

Queen ant

There are three types of ant that live in a colony—the queen, the males, and the female workers. Most colonies only have one queen. Male ants mate with the queen and then they die.

Worker ants

Most ants in a colony are female workers that cannot lay eggs. The workers collect food, build the nest, look after eggs, and feed the larvae. Soldier ants defend the colony and attack ants from other colonies.

Ant fact!

All the worker ants in a colony have the same mother, the queen, so they are all sisters!

This queen army ant has a huge abdomen and can lay thousands of eggs.

Soldier ants have huge jaws, which they use to attack predators.

Supercolonies

The largest ant colonies can cover a huge area. Argentine ants, which arrived in Europe about 80 years ago, have now formed a supercolony containing billions of ants. It stretches 3,700 miles (6,000 kilometers) along the coast from Italy to Portugal.

This female worker ant is taking a dead termite back to the nest.

Ant food

Ants eat many kinds of food, including seeds and rotting fruit that they find on the ground. Ants especially love sweet foods, such as sugar and nectar.

Squeezing out the juice

Ants cannot chew and swallow chunks of food. Instead, they use their powerful jaws to grip and squeeze the liquid out of the food. They then drink the liquid and leave the rest.

Ant fact!

African tribesmen use soldier driver ants to stitch up wounds. The soldier ant bites the wound. Then they cut off the body, leaving the head with the jaws in place.

Some ants keep "herds" of aphids that they milk to get a sugary juice called honeydew.

Ant hunters

Driver ants in Africa and army ants in South America are two of the most feared types of ant. Each day, millions of these fierce ants swarm across the forest floor on hunting raids. Thousands of animals flee for their lives as a swarm approaches.

Some of these army ants are forming "bridges" with their bodies so that other ants can march over them.

These ants are moving the body of a grasshopper back to their nest.

Spiders

Spiders belong to a group of animals called arachnids. Arachnids have four pairs of legs, eight eyes, a pair of fangs, and a body divided into two parts—the head-thorax and the abdomen. Spiders' legs have joints so they can bend. Scorpions, mites, and ticks are also arachnids.

Leg

Joint

Front part (head-thorax)

Rear part (abdomen)

A spider's body is divided into two parts.

Claw

The spider's armor

The spider's body has a tough outer covering, like a suit of armor. This is called an **exoskeleton**. It protects the spider. Spiders are unusual because they can make silk. Many spiders use their silk to make webs.

All spiders have eight legs.

spider fact!

Spiders have a collection of short hairs on their feet. These allow the spider to walk upside down on ceilings and over glass.

The body and legs of a tarantula are covered in hairs.

Beginning life

This female spider has wrapped her eggs in a cocoon of silk threads.

Female spiders usually lay their eggs at night. Some female spiders lay a small number of large eggs, while others produce thousands of eggs. All spiders lay their eggs inside a protective cocoon made of silk.

spider fact!

Some spiders can lay 1,000 eggs in less than ten minutes.

Hatching

The spider larvae hatch from the eggs at the same time. They break out of the eggs using a special egg tooth. They stay inside the cocoon until they have grown larger and it is safe for them to leave.

Spiderlings are tiny when they hatch from the eggs.

Moving on

With some species of spiders, the spiderlings move onto a special nursery web made by their mother. Some female spiders catch prey for their young to eat. After several weeks, the spiderlings move away and live on their own.

Wolf spiders make a nursery web for their spiderlings.

Spinning webs

Many spiders make a web to catch their prey. A spider starts by spinning a thread that becomes attached to a branch. Then it lays another thread to form a "Y" shape. The spider then moves to the middle and spins threads that look like the spokes of a wheel. Finally, the spider lays a sticky thread in a spiral from the middle to the outside. It is this sticky thread that catches the prey.

Orb web spiders often place their webs across en spaces between bushes to trap flying insects.

spider fact!

Some species eat their old web before starting a new one. Others roll up their web into a tiny ball and throw it away.

Catching prey

Many spiders wait in the middle of their web. Any prey flying into the web gets stuck on the sticky threads. When the prey struggles, it makes vibrations. The spider feels these vibrations and rushes over to catch the prey before it can struggle free.

Banana or Nephila spiders spin huge webs that stretch several yards across.

Glossary

Abdomen The rear part of an insect or arachnid's body.

Adapted An animal that has changed to suit the environment in which it lives.

Ancient Very old.

Antennae Feelers that detect smells in the air.

Bird of prey A bird that hunts and eats small animals.

Blowhole The nostril of a whale, dolphin, or porpoise on top of its head.

Blubber A thick layer of fat under the skin.

Breaching When a whale jumps above the surface of the water.

Calf The name for a baby or young whale, elephant, and giraffe.

Camouflage An animal's coloring that blends in with the background and makes them difficult to see.

Carnivore An animal that hunts and eats other animals.

Caterpillar The wormlike, growing stage in the life cycle of a butterfly.

Cetacean A group of marine animals that includes whales, dolphins, and porpoises.

Chrysalis (also called the pupa) The structure in which the body of a larva turns into an adult.

Clutch A batch of eggs laid at the same time by a female.

Cocoon A case made of silk spun by spiders to protect their eggs, and a protective case for butterfly larvae during metamorphosis.

Colony A group of individuals living together.

Cow The female of a species such as elephant, dolphin, and giraffe.

Den A safe, warm hiding place such as a cave or a hollow under a fallen tree.

Echolocation A special ability to "see" using sound.

Exoskeleton The tough outer covering of insects and spiders that protects their body.

Eyrie An eagle's nest.

Gills Organs inside the body of a fish or tadpole used for breathing in water.

Hatch To break out of an egg.

Hatchling A young turtle or crocodile that has just emerged from the egg.

Herbivore An animal that eats plants.

Hibernation When an animal goes into a deep sleep during the cold winter months.

Incubate To keep eggs warm so the chicks inside will grow.

Insect An animal with three body parts—head, thorax, and abdomen—with three pairs of legs and usually two pairs of wings.

Invertebrate An animal without a backbone.

Krill Small, shrimplike animals eaten by whales and penguins.

Larva The growing stage between an egg and a pupa.

Latin An old language spoken by the ancient Romans.

Litter Two or more young animals born together, to one mother.

Mammal An animal that gives birth to live young and feeds newborns with milk.

Mandibles An insect's jaws, used for biting and crushing food.

Mate To pair or breed.

Metamorphosis The changes that take place in some animals between the larva and adult stage.

Migration A journey an animal takes each year to find food or to breed.

Molt To shed an exoskelton and replace it with a new, larger one.

Nectar The sugary liquid produced by many flowers.

Omnivore An animal that eats a mixed diet of animal and plant food.

Pectoral fin Fin that is positioned just behind the gill slits in fish.

Pod A family group of whales, dolphins, or porpoises.

Pollen A powder produced by flowers.

Predator An animal that hunts other animals for food.

Pregnant A female animal that has a baby or babies developing inside.

Prey An animal that is hunted by a predator.

Primate A type of mammal that has hands and feet and a large brain.

Proboscis The feeding tube of certain insects.

Pupa Structure in which the body of the larva develops into an adult.

Rain forest Dense forest found in hot and wet parts of the world.

Reptile An animal with scaly skin, such as a crocodile or snake.

Shoal A group of fish.

Silverback A fully grown male gorilla that leads the family group.

Skull Bones in the head that protect the brain.

Sonar A device used by submarines and ships to find objects in water and calculate how far away they are.

Streamlined Having a smooth shape that slips easily through water.

Suckle When baby animals feed on their mother's milk.

Talon The curved claw of a bird of prey, such as an eagle.

Territory An area in which an animal spends its life and where it finds all its food and water.

Thermal A current of warm air that rises into the air.

Thorax The second part of the body of an insect, joining the head to the abdomen.

Trunk The very long nose of the elephant.

Webbed Having thin flaps of skin between the toes of the feet.

Wingspan The distance from the tip of one of a bird's wings to the tip of the other.

Index

alligators 70–77
American alligator 71, 74
American black bear 27
amphibians 78–83
antennae 90, 102
ants 102–107
apes 8–14
arachnids 108
Argentine ant 105
army ants 107
Australian freshwater crocodile 70, 74

bald eagle 58
baleen whales 21
banana spider 113
barn owls 57
bateleur eagle 60
bats 4–7
beaks 52, 54, 55
bears 26–29
bees 96–101
big cats 30–39

birds 48
birds of prey 54–61
black ant 104
black bear 27
blowhole 18
blubber 23
blue morpho butterfly 92, 93
blue shark 84
blue whale 17, 21
bottlenose dolphin 17, 18
breathing 36
brown bear 27, 29
Burmese python 68
butterflies 90–95

Cagle's map turtle 62
camouflage 59, 94–95
cane toad 78
carnivores 20, 28, 30, 38–39

caterpillars 92–93, 94
cats 30–39
cheetah 30, 31, 32, 36–37, 38
chimpanzee 8, 13
Chinstrap penguin 49
chrysalis 92–93
cocoon 92, 110, 111
comma butterfly 94
common egg-eater snake 67
common frog 82, 83
crocodiles 70–77
cubs,
    bear 26, 27, 29
    big cat 32, 34–35
    lion 30, 33

Darwin's frog 81
deadleaf butterfly 95
desert tortoise 65

digestion 77
dogfish 86
dolphins 16–25
driver ants 107

eagles 54
echolocation 6, 25
elephants 40–43
Emperor penguin 49
exoskeleton 109
eyelash viper 69
eyrie 56

falcons 54
feathers 48, 58, 59
fins 84
fish-eating bat 7
flippers 17, 53
flying 5, 58-59, 90, 98
frogs 78–83
frog spawn 80
fur 26

garden ant 106
gills 17, 82, 84
giraffes 44–47

glass frog 81
Goliath frog 79
gorillas 8–9, 10–11, 12–13
great horned owl 55
great white shark 85
green turtle 63

hawks 54
hearing 6, 24
Hector's dolphin 17
herbivores 45
herds 43, 47
hibernation 27
honeybee 98, 99
hook-nosed snake 67
horn shark 88
humans 8
Humboldt penguin 52
humpback whale 20

incubation 50
Indus River dolphin 19

insects 90, 96, 102
invertebrates 88, 96

killer whale 23
king penguin 48, 49, 52
krill 21, 52

larvae 98, 100, 103
leatherback turtle 62, 65
lions 30, 32, 33, 39
lungs 17, 36, 82

mandibles 102
metamorphosis 93, 99, 103
midwife toad 81
migration 23
milk 10, 16, 19, 26, 32, 42
molting 92
monarch butterfly 95
morpho butterfly 90

nectar 6, 91, 97, 106
nephila spider 113

newts 78
Nile crocodile 75, 76

omnivores 29
orangutan 8–9,
    10–11, 13, 14
orb web spider
    112–113
orcas 21, 23
orchard swallowtail
    94
owls 54, 55

penguins 48–53
pipistrelle bat 7
poisons 95
polar bear 27, 28
pollen 96, 97, 98,
    100
porpoises 16–25
pride 30, 33
primates 8
proboscis 91
pupae 98, 100, 103
pythons 68

rain forests 9, 13
reptiles 62, 66, 70

reticulated python
    68
roosts 5

salamanders 78
saliva 45
sand tiger shark 89
scales 71
sea snakes 66
seals 28
senses 24–25
sharks 84–89
shoal 20
silk 109, 110
silverbacks 9, 12
skull 24
sleep 47
smell 41
snakes 66–69
snowy owl 59, 61
soldier ants 104,
    105, 107
sonar 25
spiders 108–113
spinner dolphin 22
spiny shark 87
Steller's sea eagle
    60

swallowtail 93

tadpoles 82–83
talons 54, 55
territory 35
Thomson's gazelle
    38
thorax 90, 96, 108
tigers 30, 31, 32, 33,
    39
toads 78–83
tortoises 65
tree frog 79, 81, 83
trunks 40–41
turtles 62–65
tusks 40

Verraux's eagle 54
vultures 54

warning colors 95
wasps 96–101
webs 112–113
whales 16–25
wings 58, 90, 93
wolf spider 111
wood ants 104